BABY BEARS
and How They Grow

A shy black bear cub peeks from behind a pine tree.

by Jane Heath Buxton

BOOKS FOR YOUNG EXPLORERS
NATIONAL GEOGRAPHIC SOCIETY

Snow covers the cold ground, and black bears are cozy in their dens. A baby bear lies close to its mother. It was born in the middle of winter. At first, the cub was very small and had almost no hair. Its eyes were closed, like a newborn puppy's.

A mother bear usually has two or three cubs at a time. They grow fast, drinking her milk while she rests.

A mother black bear gives her cub a gentle lick. Nearly four months old, the cub has begun to explore the world outside the den. Cubs stay close to their mother as she looks for food. They will drink her milk for a few more months. Then they will eat different kinds of food. In spring bears find grasses and other plants in the woods.

A young black bear looks for juicy berries among the leaves.
It sniffs out the berries and uncovers them with its big paw.
Lying back, a lazy-looking cub lifts some grass to its mouth.
A grasshopper hiding in the grass can also make a good snack.
Bears often eat insects such as grasshoppers, ants, and bees.
A hungry bear may even turn over rocks to look for insects.

Soon after leaving the den, black bear cubs learn to climb trees. Their strong, sharp claws dig into the bark.

The cubs move quickly up a tree if there is any danger. High in the branches, cubs play and look around. Their mother watches out for them below. When it is safe, she calls to the cubs. They back down the tree, tail first.

Young polar bears follow
their mother over ice and snow
in the cold far north. Thick fur
and the fat under their skin
help keep them warm.

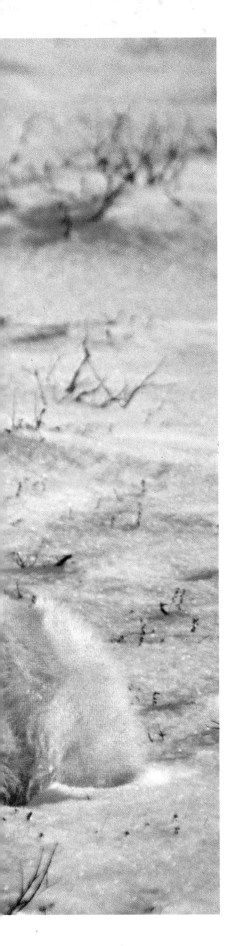

Polar bear cubs stay with their mother for two years. She sometimes nurses her cubs sitting up. Polar bears are born in winter in dens dug out of the snow. A fluffy white cub, three months old, is about as large as a house cat. After a meal, cubs snuggle up and use their mother for a pillow.

Young polar bears fight playfully. They are learning how to protect themselves when they are on their own. Tired out, the bears lie down and rest, side by side.

Looking and sniffing for food, an adult polar bear walks over the ice. The huge bear can smell a seal far away.
A polar bear spends most of its life alone, hunting seals on the sea ice.

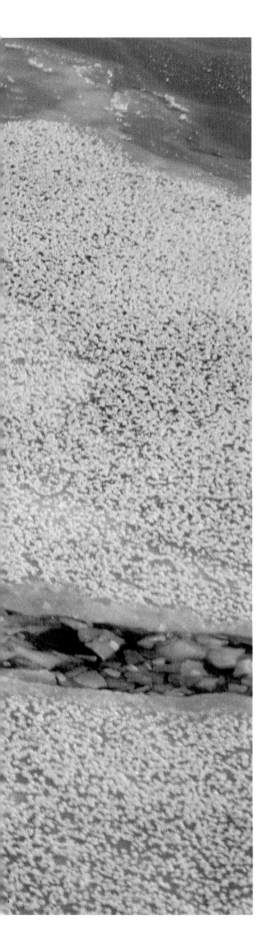

Paddling like a dog, a polar bear breaks through the ice as it swims. This ice is too thin to hold the heavy animal. The bear may swim under the water until it finds thicker ice to climb onto. To breathe, it pokes holes through the ice with its large head.

Holding its head above water, a polar bear paddles with its strong front legs. It can easily swim a hundred miles without stopping.

Young bears are curious about other animals around them. This grizzly cub is chasing a small furry animal that has white stripes on its back. What do you think is going to happen?

When the cub gets ahead and turns around, the skunk stops. It waves its bushy tail in warning. In a moment, it might spray a stinky mist. This time, both skunk and bear take off. Older bears know better than to get too near a skunk.

In late summer, big fish called salmon swim up this river to lay their eggs. Brown bears come to the waterfall to go fishing. The biggest and strongest get the best places to fish.

Bears gather in groups along rivers full of fish or among bushes thick with berries. But most of the time, they stay alone. Holding a fish in its paws, a bear bites off pieces with its sharp teeth.

Watching their mother, young brown bears learn how to fish. She wades into the water and looks around. Quick as a flash, she catches a salmon in her strong jaws.

The mother bear brings the fish to her cubs. They are not yet ready to find their own food. Sea gulls swoop down to eat the leftovers.

One bear swats another in a play fight.
On a hot summer day, a bear floats on its back
in the river. A tasty fish may soon swim by.
From a lookout rock, a brown bear sees
a salmon and dives after it. The bear will use
its big paws to hold the slippery fish.

He swung himself into the saddle and took his spear from the Boy. "Now don't be afraid," he added kindly. "I've marked my spot exactly, and *he's* sure to give me all the assistance in his power, because he knows it's his only chance of being asked to the banquet!"

St. George now shortened his spear, bringing the butt well up under his arm; and, instead of galloping as before, trotted smartly towards the dragon, who crouched at his approach, flicking his tail till it cracked in the air like a great cart whip. The Saint wheeled as he neared his opponent and circled warily round him, keeping his eye on the spare place; while the dragon, adopting similar tactics, paced with caution round the same circle, occasionally feinting with his head. So the two sparred for an opening, while the spectators maintained a breathless silence.

Though the round lasted for some minutes, the end was so swift that all the Boy saw was a lightning movement of the Saint's arm, and then a whirl and a confusion of spines, claws, tail, and flying bits of turf. The dust cleared away, the spectators whooped and ran in cheering, and the Boy made out that the dragon was down, pinned to the earth by the spear, while St. George had dismounted, and stood astride of him.

It all seemed so genuine that the Boy ran in breathlessly, hoping the dear old dragon wasn't really hurt. As he approached, the dragon lifted one large eyelid, winked solemnly, and collapsed again. He was held fast to earth by the neck, but the Saint had hit him in the spare place agreed upon, and it didn't even seem to tickle.

"Bain't you goin' to cut 'is 'ed orf, master?" asked one of the applauding crowd. He had backed the dragon, and naturally felt a trifle sore.

"Well, not *today*, I think," replied St. George, pleasantly. "You see, that can be done at *any* time. There's no hurry at all. I think we'll all go down to the village first, and have some refreshment, and then I'll give him a good talking-to, and you'll find he'll be a very different dragon!"

The Flower Queen's Daughter

retold by Andrew Lang

A YOUNG PRINCE was riding one day through a meadow that stretched for miles in front of him, when he came to a deep open ditch. He was turning aside to avoid it, when he heard the sound of someone crying in the ditch. He dismounted from his horse, and stepped along in the direction the sound came from. To his astonishment he found an old woman, who begged him to help her out of the ditch. The Prince bent down and lifted her out of her living grave, asking her at the same time how she had managed to get there.

"My son," answered the old woman, "I am a very poor woman, and soon after midnight I set out for the neighboring town in order to sell my eggs in the market on the following morning; but I lost my way in the dark, and fell into this deep ditch, where I might have remained for ever but for your kindness."

Then the Prince said to her, "You can hardly walk; I will put you on my horse and lead you home. Where do you live?"

"Over there, at the edge of the forest in the little hut you see in the distance," replied the old woman.

The Prince lifted her on to his horse, and soon they reached the hut, where the old woman got down, and turning to the Prince said, "Just wait a moment, and I will give you something." And she disappeared into her hut, but returned very soon and said, "You are a mighty Prince, but at the same time you have a kind heart, which deserves to be rewarded. Would you like to have the most beautiful woman in the world for your wife?"

"Most certainly I would," replied the Prince.

So the old woman continued, "The most beautiful woman in the whole world is the daughter of the Queen of the Flowers, who has been captured by a dragon. If you wish to marry her, you must first set her free, and this I will help you to do. I will give you this little bell: if you ring it once, the King of the Eagles will appear; if you ring it twice, the King of the Foxes will come to you; and if you ring it three times, you will see the King of the Fishes by your side. These will help you if you are in any difficulty. Now farewell, and heaven prosper your undertaking." She handed him the little bell, and there disappeared hut and all, as though the earth had swallowed her up.

Then it dawned on the Prince that he had been speaking to a good fairy, and putting the little bell carefully in his pocket, he rode home and told his father that he meant to set the daughter of the Flower Queen free, and intended setting out on the following day into the wide world in search of the maid.

So the next morning the Prince mounted his fine horse and left his home. He had roamed round the world for a whole year, and his horse had died of exhaustion, while he himself had suffered much from want and misery, but still he had come on no trace of her he was in search of. At last one day he came to a hut, in front of which sat a very old man. The Prince asked him, "Do you not know where the Dragon lives who keeps the daughter of the Flower Queen prisoner?"

"No, I do not," answered the old man. "But if you go straight along this road for a year, you will reach a hut where my father lives, and possibly he may be able to tell you."

The Prince thanked him for his information, and continued his journey for a whole year along the same road, and at the end of it came to the little hut, where he found a very old man. He asked him the same question, and the old man answered, "No, I do not know where the Dragon lives. But go straight along this road for another year, and you will come to a hut in which my father lives. I know he can tell you."

And so the Prince wandered on for another year, always on the same road, and at last reached the hut where he found the third old man. He put the same question to him as he had put to his son and grandson; but this time the old man answered, "The Dragon lives up there on the mountain, and he has just begun his year of sleep. For one whole year he is always awake, and the next he sleeps. But if you wish to see the Flower Queen's daughter go up the second mountain: the Dragon's old mother lives there, and she has a ball every night, to which the Flower Queen's daughter goes regularly."

So the Prince went up the second mountain, where he found a castle all made of gold with diamond windows. He opened the big gate leading into the courtyard, and was just going to walk in, when seven dragons rushed on him and asked him what he wanted.

The Prince replied, "I have heard so much of the beauty and kindness

of the Dragon's Mother, and would like to enter her service."

This flattering speech pleased the dragons, and the eldest of them said, "Well, you may come with me, and I will take you to the Mother Dragon."

They entered the castle and walked through twelve splendid halls, all made of gold and diamonds. In the twelfth room they found the Mother Dragon seated on a diamond throne. She was the ugliest woman under the sun, and, added to it all, she had three heads. Her appearance was a great shock to the Prince, and so was her voice, which was like the croaking of many ravens. She asked him, "Why have you come here?"

The Prince answered at once, "I have heard so much of your beauty and kindness, that I would very much like to enter your service."

"Very well," said the Mother Dragon; "but if you wish to enter my service, you must first lead my mare out to the meadow and look after her for three days; but if you don't bring her home safely every evening, we will eat you up."

The Prince undertook the task and led the mare out to the meadow. But no sooner had they reached the grass than she vanished. The Prince sought for her in vain, and at last in despair sat down on a big stone and contemplated his sad fate. As he sat thus lost in thought, he noticed an eagle flying over his head. Then he suddenly bethought him of his little bell, and taking it out of his pocket he rang it once. In a moment he heard a rustling sound in the air beside him, and the King of the Eagles sank at his feet.

"I know what you want of me," the bird said. "You are looking for the Mother Dragon's mare who is galloping about among the clouds. I will summon all the eagles of the air together, and order them to catch the mare and bring her to you." And with these words the King of the Eagles flew away. Towards evening the Prince heard a mighty rushing sound in the air, and when he looked up he saw thousands of eagles driving the mare before them. They sank at his feet on to the ground and gave the mare over to him.

Then the Prince rode home to the old Mother Dragon, who was full of wonder when she saw him, and said, "You have succeeded today in looking after my mare, and as a reward you shall come to my ball tonight." She gave him at the same time a cloak made of copper, and led him to a big room where several young he-dragons and she-dragons were dancing together. Here, too, was the Flower Queen's beautiful daughter. Her dress was woven out of the most lovely flowers in the world, and her complexion was like lilies and roses. As the Prince was dancing with her he managed to whisper in her ear, "I have come to set you free!"

Then the beautiful girl said to him, "If you succeed in bringing the mare back safely the third day, ask the Mother Dragon to give you a foal of the mare as a reward."

The ball came to an end at midnight, and early next morning the Prince again led the Mother Dragon's mare out into the meadow. But again she vanished before his eyes. Then he took out his little bell and rang it twice.

In a moment the King of the Foxes stood before him and said: "I know already what you want, and will summon all the foxes of the world together to find the mare who has hidden herself in a hill."

With these words the King of the Foxes disappeared, and in the evening many thousand foxes brought the mare to the Prince.

Then he rode home to the Mother Dragon, from whom he received this time a cloak made of silver, and again she led him to the ballroom.

The Flower Queen's daughter was delighted to see him safe and sound, and when they were dancing together she whispered in his ear: "If you succeed again tomorrow, wait for me with the foal in the meadow. After the ball we will fly away together."

On the third day the Prince led the mare to the meadow again; but once more she vanished before his eyes. The Prince took out his little bell and rang it three times.

In a moment the King of the Fishes appeared, and said to him: "I know quite well what you want me to do, and I will summon all the fishes of the sea together, and tell them to bring you back the mare, who is hiding herself in a river."

Towards evening the mare was returned to him, and when he led her home to the Mother Dragon she said to him:

"You are a brave youth, and I will make you my body-servant. But what shall I give you as a reward to begin with?"

The Prince begged for a foal of the mare, which the Mother Dragon at once gave him, and over and above, a cloak made of gold, for she had fallen in love with him because he had praised her beauty.

So in the evening he appeared at the ball in his golden cloak; but before the entertainment was over he slipped away, and went straight to the stables, where he mounted his foal and rode out into the meadow to wait for the Flower Queen's daughter. Towards midnight the beautiful girl appeared, and placing her in front of him on his horse, the Prince and she flew like the wind till they reached the Flower Queen's dwelling. But the dragons had noticed their flight, and woke their brother out of his year's sleep. He flew into a terrible rage when he heard what had happened, and determined to lay siege to the Flower Queen's palace; but the Queen caused a forest of flowers as high as the sky to grow up round her dwelling, through which no one could force a way.

When the Flower Queen heard that her daughter wanted to marry the Prince, she said to him: "I will give my consent to your marriage gladly, but my daughter can only stay with you in summer. In winter, when everything is dead and the ground covered with snow, she must come and live with me in my palace underground." The Prince consented to this, and led his beautiful bride home, where the wedding was held with great pomp and magnificence. The young couple lived happily together till winter came, when the

Flower Queen's daughter departed and went home to her mother. In summer she returned to her husband, and their life of joy and happiness began again, and lasted till the approach of winter, when the Flower Queen's daughter went back again to her mother. This coming and going continued all her life long, and in spite of it they always lived happily together.

Li Chi Slays the Serpent

by Kan Pao

I N FUKIEN, IN the ancient state of Yüeh, stands the Yung mountain range, whose peaks sometimes reach a height of many miles. To the northwest there is a cleft in the mountains once inhabited by a giant serpent seventy or eighty feet long and wider than the span of ten hands. It kept the local people in a state of constant terror and had already killed many commandants from the capital city and many magistrates and officers of nearby towns. Offerings of oxen and sheep did not appease the monster. By entering men's dreams and making its wishes known through mediums, it demanded young girls of twelve or thirteen to feast on.

Helpless, the commandant and the magistrates selected daughters of bondmaids or criminals and kept them until the appointed dates. One day in the eighth month of every year, they would deliver a girl to the mouth of the monster's cave, and the serpent would come out and swallow the victim. This continued for nine years until nine girls had been devoured.

In the tenth year the officials had again begun to look for a girl to hold in readiness for the appointed time. A man of Chiang Lo county, Li Tan, had raised six daughters and no sons. Chi, his youngest girl, responded to the search for a victim by volunteering. Her parents refused to allow it, but she said, "Dear parents, you have no one to depend on, for having brought forth six daughters and not a single son, it is as if you were childless. I could never compare with Ti Jung of the Han Dynasty, who offered herself as a bondmaid to the emperor in exchange for her father's life. I cannot take care of you in your old age; I only waste your good food and clothes. Since I'm no use to you alive, why shouldn't I give up my life a little sooner? What could be wrong in selling me to gain a bit of money for yourselves?" But the father and mother loved her too much to consent, so she went in secret.

The volunteer then asked the authorities for a sharp sword and a snake-hunting dog. When the appointed day of the eighth month arrived, she seated herself in the temple, clutching the sword and leading the dog. First she took several pecks of rice balls moistened with malt sugar and placed them at the mouth of the serpent's cave.

The serpent appeared. Its head was as large as a rice barrel; its eyes were like mirrors two feet across. Smelling the fragrance of the rice balls, it opened its mouth to eat them. Then Li Chi unleashed the snake-hunting dog, which bit hard into the serpent. Li Chi herself came up from behind and scored the serpent with several deep cuts. The wounds hurt so terribly that the monster leaped into the open and died.

Li Chi went into the serpent's cave and recovered the skulls of the nine victims. She sighed as she brought them out, saying, "For your timidity you were devoured. How pitiful!" Slowly she made her way homeward.

The king of Yüeh learned of these events and made Li Chi his queen. He appointed her father magistrate of Chiang Lo county, and her mother and elder sisters were given riches. From that time forth, the district was free of monsters. Ballads celebrating Li Chi survive to this day.

Bilbo Baggins
and Smaug

from *The Hobbit*

by J. R. R. Tolkien

THE SUN WAS shining when he started, but it was as dark as night in the tunnel. The light from the door, almost closed, soon faded as he went down. So silent was his going that smoke on a gentle wind could hardly have surpassed it, and he was inclined to feel a bit proud of himself as he drew near the lower door. There was only the very faintest glow to be seen.

"Old Smaug is weary and asleep," he thought. "He can't see me and he won't hear me. Cheer up Bilbo!" He had forgotten or had never heard about dragons' sense of smell. It is also an awkward fact that they can keep half an eye open watching while they sleep, if they are suspicious.

Smaug certainly looked fast asleep, almost dead and dark, with scarcely a snore more than a whiff of unseen steam, when Bilbo peeped once more from the entrance. He was just about to step out on to the floor when he caught a sudden thin and piercing ray of red from under the dropping lid of Smaug's left eye. He was only pretending to sleep! He was watching the tunnel entrance! Hurriedly Bilbo stepped back and blessed the luck of his ring. Then Smaug spoke.

"Well, thief! I smell you and I feel your air. I hear your breath. Come along! Help yourself again, there is plenty and to spare!"

But Bilbo was not quite so unlearned in dragon-lore as all that, and if Smaug hoped to get him to come nearer so easily he was disappointed. "No thank you, O Smaug the Tremendous!" he replied. "I did not come for presents. I only wished to have a look at you and see if you were truly as great as tales say. I did not believe them."

"Do you now?" said the dragon somewhat flattered, even though he did not believe a word of it.

"Truly songs and tales fall utterly short of the reality, O Smaug the Chiefest and Greatest of Calamities," replied Bilbo.

"You have nice manners for a thief and a liar," said the dragon. "You seem familiar with my name, but I don't seem to remember smelling you before. Who are you and where do you come from, may I ask?"

"You may indeed! I come from under the hill, and under the hills and over the hills my paths led. And through the air. I am he that walks unseen."

"So I can well believe," said Smaug, "but that is hardly your usual name."

"I am the clue-finder, the web-cutter, the stinging fly. I was chosen for the lucky number."

"Lovely titles!" sneered the dragon. "But lucky numbers don't always come off."

"I am he that buries his friends alive and drowns them and draws them

alive again from the water. I came from the end of a bag, but no bag went over me."

"These don't sound so creditable," scoffed Smaug.

"I am the friend of bears and the guest of eagles. I am Ringwinner and Luckwearer; and I am Barrel-rider," went on Bilbo beginning to be pleased with his riddling.

"That's better!" said Smaug. "But don't let your imagination run away with you!"

This of course is the way to talk to dragons, if you don't want to reveal your proper name (which is wise), and don't want to infuriate them by a flat refusal (which is also very wise). No dragon can resist the fascination of riddling talk and of wasting time trying to understand it. There was a lot here which Smaug did not understand at all, but he thought he understood enough, and he chuckled in his wicked inside.

"I thought so last night," he smiled to himself, "Lake-men, some nasty scheme of those miserable tub-trading Lake-men, or I'm a lizard. I haven't been down that way for an age and an age; but I will soon alter that!"

"Very well, O Barrel-rider!" he said aloud. "Maybe Barrel was your pony's name; and maybe not, though it was fat enough. You may walk unseen, but you did not walk all the way. Let me tell you I ate six ponies last night and I shall catch and eat all the others before long. In return for the excellent meal I will give you one piece of advice for your good: don't have more to do with dwarves than you can help!"

"Dwarves!" said Bilbo in pretended surprise.

"Don't talk to me!" said Smaug. "I know the smell (and taste) of dwarf—no one better. Don't tell me that I can eat a dwarf-ridden pony and not know it! You'll come to a bad end, if you go with such friends, Thief Barrel-rider. I don't mind if you go back and tell them so from me." But he did not tell Bilbo that there was one smell he could not make out at all,

her keep the broken pieces of the sword, to make a new sword for his son, and that blade should be called *Gram.*

Then he died. And his wife called her maid to her and said, "Let us change clothes, and you shall be called by my name, and I by yours, lest the enemy finds us."

So this was done, and they hid in a wood, but there some strangers met them and carried them off in a ship to Denmark. And when they were brought before the King, he thought the maid looked like a Queen, and the Queen like a maid. So he asked the Queen, "How do you know in the dark of night whether the hours are wearing to the morning?"

And she said:

"I know because, when I was younger, I used to have to rise and light the fires, and still I waken at the same time."

"A strange Queen to light the fires," thought the King.

Then he asked the Queen, who was dressed like a maid, "How do you know in the dark of night whether the hours are wearing near the dawn?"

"My father gave me a gold ring," said she, "and always, ere the dawning, it grows cold on my finger."

"A rich house where the maids wore gold," said the King. "Truly you are no maid, but a King's daughter."

So he treated her royally, and as time went on she had a son called Sigurd, a beautiful boy and very strong. He had a tutor to be with him, and once the tutor bade him go to the King and ask for a horse.

"Choose a horse for yourself," said the King; and Sigurd went to the wood, and there he met an old man with a white beard, and said, "Come! Help me in horse-choosing."

Then the old man said, "Drive all the horses into the river, and choose the one that swims across."

So Sigurd drove them, and only one swam across. Sigurd chose him: his name was Grani, and he came of Sleipnir's breed, and was the best horse in the world. For Sleipnir was the horse of Odin, the God of the North, and was as swift as the wind.

But a day or two later his tutor said to Sigurd, "There is a great treasure of gold hidden not far from here, and it would become you to win it."

But Sigurd answered, "I have heard stories of that treasure, and I know that the dragon Fafnir guards it, and he is so huge and wicked that no man dares to go near him."

"He is no bigger than other dragons," said the tutor, "and if you were as brave as your father you would not fear him."

"I am no coward," says Sigurd; "why do you want me to fight with this dragon?"

Then his tutor, whose name was Regin, told him that all this great hoard of red gold had once belonged to his own father. And his father had three sons—the first was Fafnir, the Dragon; the next was Otter, who could put on the shape of an otter when he liked; and the next was himself, Regin, and he was a great smith and maker of swords.

Now there was at that time a dwarf called Andvari, who lived in a pool beneath a waterfall, and there he had hidden a great hoard of gold. And one day Otter had been fishing there, and had killed a salmon and eaten it, and was sleeping, like an otter, on a stone. Then someone came by, and threw a stone at the otter and killed it, and flayed off the skin, and took it to the house of Otter's father. Then he knew his son was dead, and to punish the person who had killed him he said he must have the otter's skin filled with gold, and covered all over with red gold, or it should go worse with him. Then the person who had killed Otter went down and caught the Dwarf who owned all the treasure and took it from him.

Only one ring was left, which the Dwarf wore, and even that was taken from him.

Then the poor Dwarf was very angry, and he prayed that the gold might never bring any but bad luck to all the men who might own it, for ever.

Then the otter skin was filled with gold and covered with gold, all but one hair, and that was covered with the poor Dwarf's last ring.

But it brought good luck to nobody. First Fafnir, the Dragon, killed his own father, and then he went and wallowed on the gold, and would let his brother have none, and no man dared go near it.

When Sigurd heard the story he said to Regin:

"Make me a good sword that I may kill this Dragon."

So Regin made a sword, and Sigurd tried it with a blow on a lump of iron, and the sword broke.

Another sword he made, and Sigurd broke that too.

Then Sigurd went to his mother, and asked for the broken pieces of his father's blade, and gave them to Regin. And he hammered and wrought them into a new sword, so sharp that fire seemed to burn along its edges.

Sigurd tried this blade on the lump of iron, and it did not break, but split the iron in two. Then he threw a lock of wool into the river, and when it floated down against the sword it was cut into two pieces. So Sigurd said that sword would do. But before he went against the Dragon he led an army to fight the men who had killed his father, and he slew their King, and took all his wealth, and went home.

When he had been at home a few days, he rode out with Regin one morning to the heath where the Dragon used to lie. Then he saw the track which the Dragon made when he went to a cliff to drink, and the track was as if a great river had rolled along and left a deep valley.

Then Sigurd went down into that deep place, and dug many pits in it, and in one of the pits he lay hidden with his sword drawn. There he waited, and presently the earth began to shake with the weight of the Dragon as he crawled to the water. And a cloud of venom flew before him as he snorted and roared, so that it would have been death to stand before him.

But Sigurd waited till half of him had crawled over the pit, and then he thrust the sword Gram right into his very heart.

Then the Dragon lashed with his tail till stones broke and trees crashed about him.

Then he spoke, as he died, and said:

"Whoever thou art that hast slain me this gold shall be thy ruin, and the ruin of all who own it."

Sigurd said:

"I would touch none of it if by losing it I should never die. But all men die, and no brave man lets death frighten him from his desire. Die thou, Fafnir," and then Fafnir died.

And after that Sigurd was called Fafnir's Bane, and Dragonslayer.

The Story of Wang Li

by Elizabeth Coatsworth

ONCE IN CHINA many many years ago there lived a young man named Wang Li, with his old mother, on a small farm under the shadow of the Hill of the Seven Stars. When he was a boy he studied letters and charms with a famous sage who lived by himself in the Wind Cave halfway up the mountain. But when he had studied for several years he declared one morning that he would climb the rough path no more.

His mother was in despair.

"How hard have I labored without your help in the fields!" she cried. "Why, in a few years you could have called the cranes out of the sky to carry us anywhere we wished, or turned flower petals into money to buy whatever we desired! Ungrateful son! Return to your studies!"

But Wang Li only shook his head.

"I have learned all that I need," he replied. *"A big heart is better than a big house."*

Upon hearing a proverb quoted at her, Wang Li's mother grew furious, and seizing her broom, beat Wang Li over the shoulders until she was tired. He, being a filial son in most matters, waited until she had stopped, and then brought her a drink of cold water fresh from the well.

After that Wang Li helped his mother in the fields, but often he slipped away to the forests at the foot of the Hill of the Seven Stars with his bow and arrow, to wander in their green shades and perhaps bring back a hare for their dinner, until he became as expert a hunter as there was in the countryside.

So the days went by and at last there came a dry spring. Week after week passed and still no rain fell and the young rice and millet shoots stood small and yellow in the fields, and the mulberry leaves hung withered on the trees, unfit for the silkworms, and the melon vines lay brittle as straws on the baked ground. Prayers were said all day long in the Temple of the God of the Soil. Incense burned in great twisted ropes of sweetness about his nostrils, gongs were sounded before him, and offerings of fish and chickens and pork lay heaped on his altars.

But still no rain fell.

Early one morning Wang Li was wandering in the forest when he saw something above his head that looked like a flight of great swans, slowly settling down towards the clear waters of Heaven Mirror Lake. Creeping without sound through the underbrush, he at last came to a thicket at the very edge of the water, and parting the leaves with careful hands, he beheld a most beautiful sight. The creatures whom he had seen were not swans but winged maidens who were playing about on the surface, splashing the water until it shone like the crystal beads in their elaborate headdresses, shaking their white wings with a sound like music, clapping their delicate hands, and pursuing one another in sport.

It happened that during their games the most beautiful of the damsels passed close to the thicket where Wang Li was hidden. Swift as a hawk he seized one snow-white wing in his strong hand, and while the other maidens rose screaming into the air, he drew his lovely captive to the shore.

For a little while she wept, but glancing at him through her lashes, she was reassured and ceased to sob. Still holding the edge of one bright wing, he questioned her.

"What is your name, beautiful one?" he asked.

"I am called the Sky Damsel and am the youngest daughter of the Cloud Dragon," she answered timidly. And then went on: "You are the first human being I have ever seen. If you will come with me I will take you to the sixteen palaces of my father that are built upon the clouds. One palace is of white jade and silver, and butterflies guard the gates; another palace is built of marble inlaid with rose quartz, and its gardens are famous for their peonies; another palace has walls of gold, and is overlooked by a high pagoda on which stands the bird of the sun to crow to the dawn; and the last palace is built of ebony with pavilions of scarlet lacquer, and Lightning stands on the left of the gate and Thunder on the right. If you will come, you shall be my husband and live in whichever palace you please, and you shall ride on steeds of vapor and pluck the stars as you pass."

"I am a poor man," said Wang Li, "and the son of a poor man. How should I live in a palace? But if I give you your freedom, Sky Damsel, will you swear to me that in return you will ask your august parent to send upon this unfortunate countryside the requisite rains, so that the crops will flour-

ish and the people may not die? And he might keep a special eye on my mother's little farm at the foot of Seven Stars Hill," he added, "for she works hard and likes her garden to do well."

"It shall be as you have said," replied the Sky Damsel, and she flew away, often looking back and weeping.

But Wang Li returned home, and as he neared his mother's house the rain began to fall, soft and warm, filling all the ditches with the gurgle of running water.

"Rejoice," cried his mother as he entered, "the drought is over! And just in time, too! Now the crops will be spared. I wonder how it occurred?"

"Oh, I know all about *that*," said Wang Li, and he told her what had happened by the lonely shore of Heaven Mirror Lake.

At once his mother flew into a rage.

"And you only asked for rain," she screamed, "when we might have lived in palaces, and worn silk woven from moonlight, and fed on the fruit of the immortals! Oh, you undutiful son!"

And she fell to beating him with her broom. But when at last she stopped exhausted, he only remarked:

"A chicken coop is still a chicken coop even when covered with a cloth of gold." And he lifted a pot of dumplings which was in danger of boiling over.

Now the next year it happened that Roving Horse River was in flood, spreading out over its banks, ruining fields, and carrying away houses. Its waters came up nearly to the door of the cottage where Wang Li and his mother lived, and threatened her mulberry trees. She was in despair and wept bitterly, but Wang Li took his bow and arrow from the wall.

"Are you going hunting at such a time?" she screamed. "Oh, that I should have borne a son with no heart!"

But he only said: *"If you know how, a thing is not hard; if it is hard, then you don't know how.*" And he left her with her mouth open, not understanding what he meant.

"I wish that boy would stop quoting proverbs," she muttered to herself. "He is as clever a boy as ever breathed, but what good does it do us?"

Meantime Wang Li walked along beside the bank of the river. And he saw the flood coming down in a great white wave. And having very keen eyes he saw in the midst of the wave a youth and a maiden, clothed in garments of white silk, riding white horses with silver bits. And attendants on white horses followed them.

Then Wang Li drew his bow, fitted an arrow into the string, and let it fly straight into the heart of the young man, who fell dead from his horse. At that the others turned their horses and rode away at full speed, and the flood receded with them.

But as they rode, Wang Li sent another arrow after them, which pierced the high headdress of the noble lady and shone there like a long ornament. And after a few paces, she reined in her horse and slowly rode back to where Wang Li stood.

"Here is your arrow," she said, giving it to him. "I suppose I should thank you for not sending it through my heart as you did through my cousin's, the Prince of Roving Horse River."

"I could never do anything so discourteous," murmured Wang Li.

The lady regarded him for a long time.

"Since you have spared my person," she said, "I suppose it should be yours. If you will come with me you shall be my husband, and reign in the palaces of the River Dragons. You shall sit on a throne of coral in halls of jade and crystal, and the River Maidens shall dance before you the Dance of the Ripples, and the River Warriors shall dance to please you the Dance of the Tempest."

"And what will happen to the countryside while they dance?" asked Wang Li. "No, no, I am a poor man and the son of a poor man. What should I do in palaces? If you wish to show your gratitude, make me a pledge that the river shall hereafter stay within its banks, and perhaps you might be especially careful along the edge of my mother's farm, for she is a poor woman and it grieves her to see her work washed away."

The lady raised her hand in agreement, and turned her horse, and rode off. But before she disappeared forever, she looked back for a last glimpse of Wang Li, and he saw that she was weeping. A little sad, he returned to his mother's house and, as he walked, he noticed how the waters were draining off the land, leaving behind them, as tribute, pools filled with round-mouthed fish.

His mother met him at the door.

"See! See!" she cried, "the waters are withdrawing! But you, you wicked son, you left me here to drown and little you cared!"

"Indeed, I only went to bring you help!" said Wang Li, and he told his mother all that had happened. At hearing the story she nearly choked with rage.

"What! We might have lived in river palaces and dined off turtle eggs and carps' tongues every day!" she cried. "And I might have ridden on a dragon forty feet long when I went calling! All this might have been mine but you refused it, you ungrateful son!" And she seized her broom.

Whack!

"Take that!"

Whack!

"And that!"

Whack! Whack! Whack!

"And that! And that! And that!"

But when at last her arm fell, Wang Li politely helped her to her chair and brought her a fan.

"Peace in a thatched hut—that is happiness," he said, once more quoting an old proverb.

"Be off with you!" replied his mother. "You are a wicked, ungrateful son and have no right to be using the words of wise men. Besides, they hadn't been offered palaces, I'm sure."

So the months passed and the rain fell when it was needed, and the river remained within its banks and reflected on its smooth waters the sun by day and the moon by night. But after some time the country was greatly disturbed by earthquakes. People were awakened from their sleep by the tremblings of their beds, the dishes danced on the tables, sheds fell flat to the earth, and everyone waited with horror for the final quake that should bring the roofs down on their heads.

"Now," wept Wang Li's old mother, "I shall die a violent death, I who might have slept safe beside the Silver Stream of Heaven or walked in the gardens of the river, if it had not been for this great foolish son."

But Wang Li took his spear and went to the mouth of the Cave of the Evening Sun which is on the west side of the Hills of the Seven Stars. Then he looked carefully at the ground beneath his feet, which was rounded up as though a huge mole had passed under it, and choosing a certain spot, drove his spear deep into the loosened soil.

"Whoever walks along that path again will scratch his back," he said to himself with satisfaction, and was about to return home when he noticed a beautiful girl who sat beside a rock spinning, and weeping as she spun.

"Why do you scatter the pearls of your eyes, young maiden?" asked Wang Li gently. And she, raising her tear-wet eyes to him, said:

"Alas, I am Precious Jade, the only daughter of the former Dragon King of the Mountains. But my ungrateful uncle has risen against his elder brother and imprisoned him in the innermost prison of the hills, and he has driven me out to work with unaccustomed hands, living in this coarse robe, and eating roots and berries, and sleeping under the stars."

Wang Li looked at her in her rough brown garments, and her beauty seemed like a flower bursting from its sheath.

"I think I have stopped the path of your uncle who has been disturbing us with his wanderings, and now perhaps he will stay in his cavern palaces. But for you I can do nothing, I fear, though I would gladly serve you."

At that Precious Jade looked at him shyly.

"If you would deign to take me away with you and allow me to serve your mother with my poor strength, I should no longer weep alone on this desolate mountain," she whispered.

"And what gifts would you bring my mother if I took you home as a bride?" asked Wang Li.

Then Precious Jade wrung her hands. "Alas," she said, "I have no gifts but only my will to serve you both." And she wept very bitterly.

At that Wang Li laughed and lifted her up in his arms and carried her home to his mother.

"Mercy!" cried the old woman, "whom have we here?"

"It is Precious Jade, the daughter of the former Dragon King of the Mountains," said Wang Li, "and she has returned here to be your daughter-in-law."

The old woman was all in a flutter.

"I must have an hour to get ready before I can present myself at court. How many guests will there be at the feast, my little dove? And how many rooms shall I have in the palace? And what color are the lanterns, or does light shine from the gems themselves in the Kingdom of the Mountain Dragons?"

"Alas!" said Precious Jade, "my father is a prisoner and I am only an exile."

"Pshaw!" exclaimed the old woman, "what a daughter-in-law for you to bring back, you senseless oaf! Look at the robe she is wearing, and her hands are fit for nothing! Go and bring me a pail of water, you useless girl! As for you," she cried, turning to her son, "you shall feel if my old arms are withered yet!" And she caught up her broom and began belaboring him with it.

"*A thin horse has long hair,*" remarked Wang Li philosophically when she had done, and he went out into the garden to find her a peach to refresh her after so much effort.

"I shall have to make the best of it," she grumbled to herself, when she had eaten the peach. "The boy has ears of stone. He follows his own way. If the mountain will not turn, I must be the road and do the turning myself." After that she was kind to Precious Jade, who tried to be of help to her mother-in-law in every possible way.

So they lived together in peace and happiness, working hard, incurring no debts, and showing kindness to all. Throughout the district the rains fell punctually, no one had any complaint of Roving Horse River, and the earth was no longer shaken by the burrowing of dragons. In time Precious Jade bore a beautiful son whom they named Little Splendor and there were never four happier people in the world. One day, not long afterwards, as Wang Li and Precious Jade sat alone beneath a grapevine trellis which Wang Li had recently made, Precious Jade began, laying down her embroidery:

"My dear husband, a message has reached me from my father. It seems that my unworthy uncle, issuing forth hastily from his palace, struck himself against the point of your spear and after some time died. My father is again on his jewel throne, and naturally feels a deep gratitude towards you." She paused.

"Now you are going to tell me about the palaces under the mountains which I may have for the asking," said Wang Li.

"I always hated palaces. There was never anything to do," said Precious Jade, smiling. Then she went back to her embroidery.

"My husband is the proudest man in the world," she remarked to a yellow silk butterfly which she had not quite finished.

"Proud?" asked Wang Li, "yet here I am and I might be a prince."

"You're too proud to be a prince," she replied, "and that is why I love you. I always wanted to marry the proudest man in the world."

"Maybe it's pride and maybe it's wisdom," said Wang Li, "but there are palaces and terraces of the mind I would not exchange for all the riches of the dragons."

And Precious Jade understood. In time Wang Li became so famous for his wisdom and benevolence that sages traveled from the farthest provinces to walk with him as he followed his plow. But sometimes when he was busy and the old mother needed a new silk gown or the baby wanted sweetmeats, Precious Jade would softly shake the leaves of the tree beside the door, and down would fall a light shower of silver coins. And Wang Li never noticed what it was that Precious Jade gathered under the mulberry tree.

St. George
and the Dragon

retold by William H. G. Kingston

THE HERMIT WELCOMED St. George and De Fistycuff. He was a venerable man, with a long beard of silvery whiteness; and as he tottered forward he seemed bowed almost to the ground with the weight of years.

"Gladly will I afford you shelter and such food as my cell can furnish, most gallant Knight," he said; and, suiting the action to the word, he placed a variety of provisions on the table. "I need not inquire to what country you belong, for I see by the arms of England engraven on your burgonet whence you come. I know the knights of that land are brave and gallant, and ready to do battle in aid of the distressed. Here, then, you will find an opportunity for distinguishing yourself by a deed which will make your name renowned throughout the world."

St. George pricked up his ears at this, and eagerly inquired what it was. "This, you must understand, most noble Knight, is the renowned territory of Bagabornabou, second to none in the world in importance in the opinion of its inhabitants. None was so prosperous, none so flourishing, when a most horrible misfortune befell the land, in the appearance of a terrific green dragon, of huge proportions, who ranges up and down the country, creating devastation and dismay in every direction. No corner of the land is safe from his ravages; no one can hope to escape the consequences of his appearance. Every day his insatiable maw must be fed with the body of a young maiden, while so pestiferous is the breath which exhales from his throat that it causes a plague of a character so violent that whole districts have been depopulated by it. He commences his career of destruction at dawn every morning, and till his victim is ready he continues to ravage the land. When he has swallowed his lamentable repast he remains asleep till next morning, and then he proceeds as before.

"Many attempts have been made to capture him during the night, but he has invariably destroyed the brave men who have gone out to attack him, and has swallowed them for his supper. For no less than twenty-four long years has this dreadful infliction been suffered by our beloved country, till scarcely a maiden remains alive, nor does a brave man continue in it. The most lovely and perfect of her sex, the King's only daughter, the charming Sabra, is to be made an offering to the fell dragon tomorrow, unless a knight can be found gallant and brave enough to risk his life in mortal combat with the monster, and with skill and strength sufficient to destroy him.

"The King has promised, in his royal word, that, should such a knight appear and come off victorious, he will give him his daughter in marriage and the crown of Bagabornabou at his decease."

"Ah!" exclaimed the English Knight, his whole countenance beaming with satisfaction, "here is a deed to be done truly worthy of my prowess! I fully purpose to kill the dragon and rescue the Princess."

The daring Knight and his faithful Squire now entered the valley where the terrific green dragon had his abode. No sooner did the fiery eyes of the hideous monster fall on the steel-clad warrior instead of the fair maiden he expected to see, than from his leathern throat he sent forth a cry of rage louder and more tremendous than thunder, and arousing himself he prepared for the contest about to occur. As he reared up on his hind legs—with his wings outspread, and his long scaly tail, with a huge red fork, extending far away behind him, his sharp claws wide open, each of the size of a large ship's anchor, his gaping mouth armed with double rows of huge teeth, between which appeared a fiery red tongue, and vast eyes blazing like burning coals, while his nostrils spouted forth fire, and the upper part of his body was covered with glittering green scales brighter than polished silver, and harder than brass, the under part being of a deep golden hue—his appearance might well have made even one of the bravest of men unwilling to attack him.

St. George trembled not, but thought of the lovely Sabra, and nerved himself for the encounter. De Fistycuff did not like his looks, and had he been alone would have been tempted to beat a retreat, but his love for his master kept him by his side.

"See," said the hermit, who had come thus far, "there is the dragon! He is a monster huge and horrible; but I believe that, like other monsters, by bravery and skill he can be overcome. See, the valley is full of fruit trees! Should he wound you, and should you be faint, you will find one bearing

oranges of qualities so beneficial, that, should you be able to procure one plucked fresh from the tree, it will instantly revive you. Now, farewell! See, the brute is approaching!"

On came the monster dragon, flapping his wings, spouting fire from his nostrils, and roaring loudly with his mouth. St. George couched his sharp spear and, spurring his steed, dashed onward to the combat. So terrific was the shock that the Knight was almost hurled from his saddle, while his horse, driven back on his haunches, lay, almost crushed, beneath the monster's superincumbent weight; but both man and steed extricating themselves with marvelous agility, St. George made another thrust of his spear, with all his might, against the scaly breast of the dragon. He might as well have struck against a gate of brass.

In a moment the stout spear was shivered into a thousand fragments, and the dragon uttered a loud roar of derision. At the same time, to show what he could do, he whisked round his venomous pointed tail with so rapid a movement that he brought both man and horse to the ground.

There they lay, almost senseless from the blow, while the dragon retreated backward some hundred paces or more, with the intention of coming back with greater force than before, and completing the victory he had almost won. Happily De Fistycuff divined the monster's purpose, and seeing one of the orange trees of which the hermit had spoken, he picked an orange and hurried with it to his master.

Scarcely had the Knight tasted it than he felt his strength revive, and leaping to his feet, he gave the remainder of it to his trusty steed, on whose back instantly mounting, he stood prepared, with his famous sword Ascalon in his hand, to receive the furious charge which the dragon was about to make.

Though his spear had failed him at a pinch, his trusty falchion was true as ever; and making his horse spring forward, he struck the monster such a blow on his golden-colored breast that the point entered between the scales, inflicting a wound which made it roar with pain and rage.

Slight, however, was the advantage which the Knight thereby gained, for there issued forth from the wound so copious a stream of black gore, with an odor so terrible, that it drove him back, almost drowning him and his brave steed, while the noxious fumes, entering their nostrils, brought them both fainting and helpless to the ground.

De Fistycuff, mindful of his master's commands, narrowly eyed the dragon, to see what he was about to do. Stanching his wound with a touch of his fiery tail, he flapped his green wings, roaring hoarsely, and shook his vast body, preparatory to another attack on the Knight.

"Is that it?" cried the Squire; and running to the orange tree, whence he plucked a couple of the golden fruit, he poured the juice of one down the throat of his master, and of the other down that of Bayard. Both revived in an instant, and St. George, springing on Bayard's back, felt as fresh and ready for the fight as ever. Both had learned the importance of avoiding the dragon's tail, and when he whisked it on one side Bayard sprang to the other, and so on, backwards and forwards, nimbly avoiding the blows aimed by the venomous instrument at him or his rider.

Again and again the dragon reared itself up, attempting to drop down and crush his gallant assailant; but Bayard, with wonderful sagacity, comprehending exactly what was to be done, sprung backwards or aside each time the monster descended, and thus avoided the threatened catastrophe. Still the dragon appeared as able as ever to endure the combat. St. George saw that a strenuous effort must be made, and taking a fresh grasp of Ascalon, he spurred onward to meet the monster, who once more advanced, with outstretched wings, with the full purpose of destroying him. This time St. George kept his spurs in the horse's flanks. "Death or victory must be the result of this change," he shouted to De Fistycuff.

With Ascalon's bright point kept well before him, he drove directly at the breast of the monster. The sword struck him under the wing; through the thick flesh it went, and nothing stopped it till it pierced the monster's heart. Uttering a loud groan, which resounded through the neighboring woods and mountains, and made even the wild beasts tremble with consternation, the furious green dragon fell over on its side, when St. George, drawing his falchion from the wound, dashed on over the prostrate form of the monster, and, ere it could rise to revenge itself on its destroyer, with many a blow he severed the head from the body. So vast was the stream which flowed forth from the wound that the whole valley speedily became a lake of blood, and the river which ran down from it first gave notice, by its sanguineous hue, to the inhabitants of the neighboring districts that the noble Champion of England had slain their long-tormenting enemy.

Stan Bolovan

retold by Andrew Lang

ONCE UPON A time what happened did happen, and if it had not happened this story would never have been told.

On the outskirts of a village just where the oxen were turned out to pasture, and the pigs roamed about burrowing with their noses among the roots of the trees, there stood a small house. In the house lived a man who had a wife, and the wife was sad all day long.

"Dear wife, what is wrong with you that you hang your head like a drooping rosebud?" asked her husband one morning. "You have everything you want; why cannot you be merry like other women?"

"Leave me alone, and do not seek to know the reason," replied she,

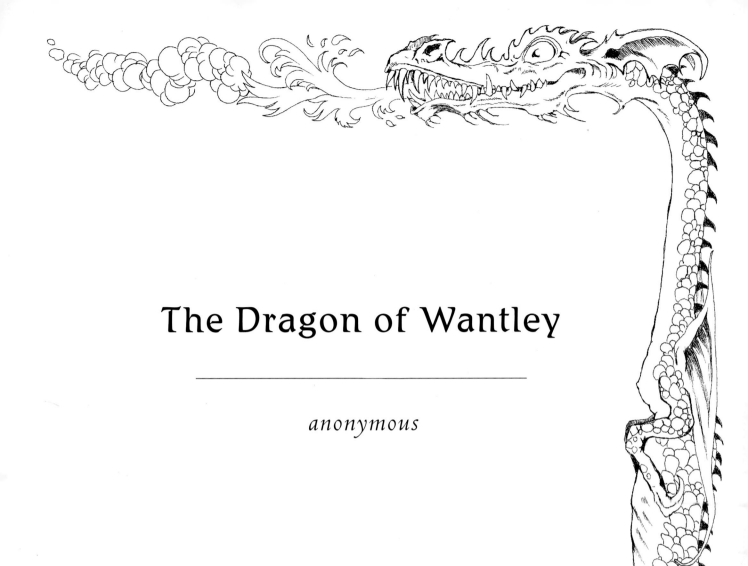

The Dragon of Wantley

anonymous

Old stories tell, how Hercules,
A dragon slew at Lerna,
With seven heads, and fourteen eyes,
To see and well discern-a:
But he had a club, this dragon to drub,
Or he had ne'er done it, I warrant ye:
But More of More Hall, with nothing at all,
He slew the dragon of Wantley.

This dragon had two furious wings,
One upon each shoulder;
With a sting in his tail, as long as a flail,
Which made him bolder and bolder.
He had long claws, and in his jaws
Four-and-forty teeth of iron;
With a hide as tough as any buff,
And as strong as the jaws of a lion.

Have you not heard how the Trojan horse
Held seventy men in his belly?
This dragon was not quite so big,
But very near, I'll tell ye.
Devoured he poor children three,
That could not with him grapple;
And at one sup he ate them up,
As one would eat an apple.

All sorts of cattle this dragon did eat:
Some say he ate up trees,
And that the forests sure he would
Devour up by degrees:
Houses and churches like geese and turkeys
He ate all and left nothing behind
But some stones, dear Jack, that he could not crack,
Which on the hills you will find.

Hard by a furious knight there dwelt,
Men, women, girls, and boys,

Sighing and sobbing, came to his lodging,
And made a hideous noise:
"O save us all, More of More Hall,
Thou peerless knight of these woods;
Do but slay this dragon, who won't leave us a rag on,
We'll give thee all our goods."

This being done, he did engage
To hew the dragon down;
But first he went new armor to
Bespeak at Sheffield town;
With spikes all about, not within but without,
Of steel so sharp and strong;
Both behind and before, arms, legs, and all o'er,
 Some five or six inches long.

Had you but seen him in this dress,
How fierce he looked and how big,
You would have thought him for to be
Some Egyptian porcupig:
He frightened all, cats, dogs, and all,
Each cow, each horse, and each hog:
For fear they did flee, for they took him to be
Some strange, outlandish hedgehog.

To see this fight all people then
Got up on trees and houses,
On churches some, and chimneys too;
But these put on their trousers,

Not to spoil their hose. As soon as he rose,
To make him strong and mighty,
He drank, by the tale, six pots of ale
And a quart of aqua vitae.

It is not strength that always wins,
For wit doth strength excel;
Which made our cunning champion
Creep down into a well;
Where he did think, this dragon would drink,
And so he did in truth;
And as he stooped low, he rose up and cried "Boo!"
And hit him in the mouth.

"Oh," quoth the dragon, "come out, my man,
Thou disturb'st me in my drink."
And then he turned and breathed fire at him:
But the brave knight did not shrink.
"Beshrew thy soul, thy body's foul,
Thy breath smells not like balsam;
Thou evil beast with stifling breath,
Sure thy diet is unwholesome."

Our politic knight, on the other side,
Crept out upon the brink,
And gave the dragon such a douse,
He knew not what to think:
"By Jove," quoth he, "say you so, do you see?"
And then at him he let fly,

With hand and with foot, and so they went to't;
And the word it was, Hey, boys, hey!

"Your words," quoth the dragon, "I don't understand."
Then to it they fell at all,
Like two wild boars so fierce, if I may
Compare great things with small.
Two days and a night, with this dragon did fight
Our champion on the ground;
Tho' their strength it was great, their skill it was neat,
They never had one wound.

At length the hard earth began to quake,
The dragon gave him a knock,
Which made him to reel, and straightway he thought,
To lift him as high as a rock,
And thence let him fall. But More of More Hall,
Life a valiant knight in his pride,
As he came like a lout, so he turned him about,
And gave him a blow in the side.

"Oh," quoth the dragon, with a deep sigh,
And turned six times together,
Sobbing and tearing, cursing and swearing
Out of his throat of leather;
"More of More Hall! O thou rascal!
Would I had seen thee never;
With the thing at thy foot, thou hast slain me at the root,
And I'm quite undone forever."

"Murder, murder," the dragon cried,
"Alack, alack for grief;
Had you but missed that place, you could
Have done me no mischief."
Then his head he shaked, trembled, and quaked,
And down he laid and cried;
First on one knee, then on back tumbled he,
So groaned, kicked, shuddered, and died.

fed at the town's expense—on whatever they liked. And they ate nothing but cakes and buns and sweet things, and they said the poor dragon was very welcome to their bread and milk.

Now, when Johnnie had been mayor ten years or so he married Tina, and on their wedding morning they went to see the dragon. He had grown quite tame, and his rusty plates had fallen off in places, and underneath he was soft and furry to stroke. So now they stroked him.

And he said, "I don't know how I could ever have liked eating anything but bread and milk. I *am* a tame dragon, now, aren't I?" And when they said yes, he was, the dragon said, "I am so tame, won't you undo me?"

And some people would have been afraid to trust him, but Johnnie and Tina were so happy on their wedding day that they could not believe any harm of anyone in the world. So they loosed the chains, and the dragon said, "Excuse me a moment, there are one or two little things I should like to fetch," and he moved off to those mysterious steps and went down them, out of sight into the darkness. And as he moved, more and more of his rusty plates fell off.

In a few minutes they heard him clanking up the steps. He brought something in his mouth—it was a bag of gold.

"It's no good to me," he said. "Perhaps you might find it come in useful." So they thanked him very kindly.

"More where that came from," said he, and fetched more and more and more, till they told him to stop. So now they were rich, and so were their fathers and mothers. Indeed, everyone was rich, and there were no more poor people in the town. And they all got rich without working, which is very wrong, but the dragon had never been to school, as you have, so he knew no better.

And as the dragon came out of the dungeon, following Johnnie and Tina into the bright gold and blue of their wedding day, he blinked his eyes as a cat does in the sunshine, and he shook himself, and the last of his plates dropped off, and his wings with them, and he was just like a very, very extra-sized cat. And from that day he grew furrier and furrier, and he was the beginning of all cats. Nothing of the dragon remained except the claws, which all cats have still, as you can easily ascertain.

And I hope you see now how important it is to feed your cat with bread and milk. If you were to let it have nothing to eat but mice and birds it might grow larger and fiercer, and scalier and tailier, and get wings and turn into the beginning of dragons. And then there would be all the bother over again.

F
BOO